This book belongs to

American Memories

NORMAN ROCKWELL

ARIEL BOOKS

ANDREWS AND McMEEL

KANSAS CITY

Frontispiece: AT THE SODA FOUNTAIN
Saturday Evening Post cover, August 22, 1953

Book design by Susan Hood

American Memories

MENDING THE FLAG

Literary Digest cover
May 27, 1922

THE OPEN ROAD

Saturday Evening Post cover
July 31, 1920

THE DEBATE

Saturday Evening Post cover
October 9, 1920

HALLOWEEN

—

Saturday Evening Post cover
October 23, 1920

POSTCARD

Saturday Evening Post cover
February 18, 1922

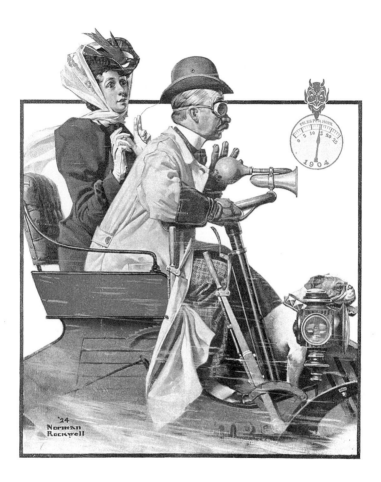

SPEED

Saturday Evening Post cover
July 19, 1924

THE TACKLE

———

Saturday Evening Post cover
November 21, 1925

UNCLE SAM TAKES WING

—

Saturday Evening Post cover
January 21, 1928

FISHING

—

Saturday Evening Post cover
August 3, 1929

STOCK EXCHANGE QUOTATIONS

Saturday Evening Post cover
January 18, 1930

FIRE!

Saturday Evening Post cover
March 28, 1931

CRAMMING

Saturday Evening Post cover
June 13, 1931

THE SPIRIT OF EDUCATION

—

Saturday Evening Post cover
April 21, 1934

STRIKING A BARGAIN

—

Saturday Evening Post cover
May 19, 1934

VACATION

———

Saturday Evening Post cover
June 30, 1934

SCHOOL DAYS

—

Saturday Evening Post cover
September 14, 1935

BARBERSHOP QUARTET

Saturday Evening Post cover
September 26, 1936

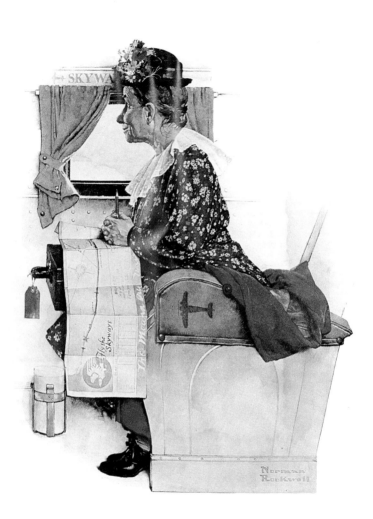

FIRST FLIGHT

Saturday Evening Post cover
June 4, 1938

THE DRUGGIST

Saturday Evening Post cover
March 18, 1939

100 YEARS OF BASEBALL

———

Saturday Evening Post cover
July 8, 1939

CENSUS TAKER

Saturday Evening Post cover
April 27, 1940

USO VOLUNTEERS

Saturday Evening Post cover
February 7, 1942

ROSIE THE RIVETER

———

Saturday Evening Post cover
May 29, 1943

WHICH ONE?

—

Saturday Evening Post cover
November 4, 1944

TAXES

—

Saturday Evening Post cover
March 17, 1945

HAPPY HOMECOMING

Saturday Evening Post cover
May 26, 1945

THANKSGIVING

———

Saturday Evening Post cover
November 24, 1945

STATUE OF LIBERTY

Saturday Evening Post cover
July 6, 1946

ELECTION DAY

Saturday Evening Post cover
October 30, 1948

BOTTOM OF THE SIXTH

Saturday Evening Post cover
April 23, 1949

EXPENSES

—

Saturday Evening Post cover
November 30, 1957

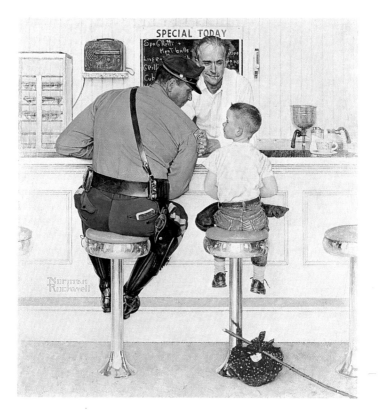

THE RUNAWAY

Saturday Evening Post cover
September 20, 1958

SAYING GRACE

───

Saturday Evening Post cover
November 24, 1951